When the Moon
Had Antlers

By

Tresha Faye Haefner

Pine Row Press

When the Moon Had Antlers

Published by Pine Row Press
Ft. Mitchell, KY 41011

ISBN: 979-8-9875064-1-7

April 2023

First Edition

10 9 8 7 6 5 4 3 2 1

=====

Cover art by Vizerskaya

Photo of poet by Alexis Rhone Fancher

Poet's website at www.thepoetrysalon.com

Publisher's website at www.pinerow.com

Table of Contents

I

II

III

IV

V

I

Why do we Pretend God isn't an Animal

A beetle antlered for the hoisting of stars?
–Brendan Constantine

When there is no light
I smell my way by the trees,
the sound of mud moving. Feel
of my body stubbing itself blind.

Bowerbirds are out there.
Singing questions. Why is this hunger?
What shall we worship?

Now I try to reconfigure myself. Wonder
what is the distance between the dirt and the darkness?
I push over trees. Force
this coal to burn into futures.

All around us is moving. We root around
for scarabs, garnets, the devil's bright horsefly.
Under our feet black rainbows gather.

We'll hoist any reflection upwards, find ourselves
on any pattern of flashes. Name the constellations
after any animal we can lose track of.

Anything to end this aloneness.
Anything to connect
our bodies back to the stars.

Spring Delayed

This world keeps remaking itself – without me.
–Kelly Grace Thomas

Something is coming, spring
or ice age. I do not know.

Winter hid me in its shimmer.
Loneliness kept company.

Now buds break. Bloodlust
for color.

Lion's mane mushrooms brighten
through branches.

Only I want the world
invisible again,

quiet enough to reconfigure myself
toward silence.

A spider, listening to stories. A cicada
lost in its hush.

But the world is remaking itself, insistent
we move forward. Listen.

The old season falls
on its sword. The sky turns red.

Something wasted is leaving the earth.
Something new is starting to bleed.

Wasted

I don't know if we are living
in a church of palms or burning
the aftermath of dinosaurs.

Along the shore of this bought-and-paid-for beach
vacation, I walk. Knife-eyed
iguanas scatter up trees.

A crab hides in the arrogance of shade.
This planet is afraid of what we want.
Tries to bronze us from without, shrivel

us with thirst from within.
Whatever I do, I fail
to start a fire from two good diplomas.

I need so much more
than this education can give.
Alcohol. Effexor. A good cry.

But no matter how many times the earth warns me,
I fill each coconut with rum. Crash
into the fists of these waves.

Our father, who art in the ocean,
We make of this danger a daring,
splay out in the sand, gilded

with sun, while the sea foam calculates.
The planet tilts. Nobody watches
our dangerous shoulders burn.

Bang

Blackbirds fell from the sky in Arkansas today.

On the coast of South Africa,
fifty-five pilot whales
beached themselves in the sand.

Consider the squirrel,
dead on the highway

and the cosmos,
how everything began like opening
a bag of potato chips.

Scientists unspool string theory
but don't know how the whales got lost.

This morning I found a rat skeleton
by the wheel of my car,
another outside the door to work.

One day my cat caught a mouse
but left it, still living, on the patio.

It breathed hard
and looked around at the eucalyptus trees.

The heaviness of a last breath seemed
immense. I couldn't take it
from the mouse. I just watched

and waited. The pressure
of the atmosphere on the lungs
was too much.

Animals know what they're doing,
but I cannot turn off
the motor in the heart, beach myself
on a lonely coast.

I look on the internet again;
more dead blackbirds,
this time in Kansas.

The scientists have gone
down to the beach
to euthanize the whales.

Some things are so heavy,
we can do nothing
to put them back where they belong.

Territorial Boundaries

See the way we pocket our sadness. Dress
in isolation. Keep the halogen on. We can see
what's coming for us.

Cars. Cable bills. The man who enters
without keys.

It's a hustle for meaning,
odd mating dance of money. Whiskeys threatened
for nine dollars apiece.

At night we throw back
the sunrise of civilization,

smell the first lemony green hops crushed
against granite. First grain rolled into bread.

It was a mistake, wasn't it?

How we separated our families
by bricks, our love by wallets.

Now the birds sing
the same warbles and whistles

they've passed down since sunlight
started them blazing.

But our ears have changed.

Is this why we affix
heads of animals on gods,
carve wings onto the backs of angels,
tattoo ourselves with feathers?

To remind us how easy we were
as animals? Everything built inside our bodies.

Claws. Sinew, a warning signal attuned
to someone else's hunger.

We wanted nothing
but days nursing
on rain.

Today deer still circle the forest.
They live in an abundance

of silence, sleeping on the wet
of winter, fur ignited by snow.
Not even waiting
for a thaw.

Dear Iceberg

My dream in life is to reach out and touch an iceberg.
–Journal entry from a boy with autism

Here is the glass moon,
hung over a table of snow.
The flower vases offering up
their ruffle of ice.

Here, iceberg, we have broken
glass. Broken ships.
Splinters of oars lost by the Romans
and the Toyota broken down
on the side of the 101.

Here, iceberg, we have whole lexicons
for loneliness. A rocket ship
that cannot reach farther
than the moon.

Iceberg, we are all speechless
wanderers. Some of us
have cell phones,
the internet and airplanes,

people who will hug us
then melt back into the night.
Iceberg, we've got mirrors
to shine back our silhouetted faces.

We've got photos
of our planet from space.
Iceberg, we've got images of you
on our laptops.

Tell me, iceberg, do you enjoy
these small dark hours,
the wordless conversation
of the aurora australis,
the whale swimming under your belly?

Iceberg, does this translate into love?
The breath of a seal on your skin,
the return of colored glare reflected
in the eye of a mother bear?

In a small room,
in a small school,
a boy we cannot understand
writes to you.

I picture him in a ship
in the southernmost part
of the planet, clad in a feathered coat
like a snow goose. Does it warm you now
to think of him, coming all that way to find you,
finally reaching
his fingers into the cold?

How to Deal with Mortality

All your life you have wanted the tattoo of a mermaid.
One perfect image on the imperfect body.
Half invention of starry-eyed sailors,
half salt-bound animal inked
into the ocean of your impermanence.

You rise disheveled, but she waits,
already formed, clutching her mermaid
shell, her arm poised like a scepter of the sea.

See how the motion of her fin flicks
the hot from her tail,
an ouroboros of form. She has nothing to regret
because she has nothing
to say. Her sound the perfect
hush of waves: voiceless.

Her eyes roll their amnesiac alibis
over an isthmus without a name.

Cartographers cross this hemisphere.
Salt dogs put their mark
where no mark belongs, but
you can look in on her always,
and she is always the same.

Map of an unchanged world.
She will never see you
grow old or hear the wind
waste through the drying seaweed of your skin.

She will never feel the sea
around herself stutter stale
or the salted freckles of your body lose
their luster.

Newly made, newly alive, she stares
at the sand minefields of the sea,
the continuous ritual of combs and mirrors,

and this is how you will live too,
startled every morning by your own beauty,
skin scarred by the color of myth,
the flesh still fresh and surprised
as a newly opened fish.

How to Identify the Body of God

who has no body.
The God whose body is glacier and apostrophe.
Whose language is lagoon and Chinook salmon swimming
  upstream.
A God who keeps hiding shells in her pocket, destroying
the dinosaurs and keeping their skeletons in tar light.

If I chase these chalices across every lunar eclipse, if I shine
like a horse and powder my eyes green, as the fins of a fighter
  fish,
if I spin myself into sunset, Ferris wheel forward
and chisel my image into the side of a church, if I follow
this scent, fill each footprint with alabaster and stone,
if I leave my tooth lodged in your heart,
can you tell me what kind of God you are?

What kind of animal I am?

II

The Jungle Tattoo

The man who lived in this apartment before me
painted the walls dark green so they would look
like the deep round 'O' of a forest pool in shade,

but really, they remind me of the man himself,
who, upon handing me the keys, had said
he had lived there ten years, alone,

that the neighbors were quiet,
but few of them friendly,
and I should keep to myself,

then had turned down the hall, revealing,
through the cotton white lucidity of his shirt,
a back covered by the tattoo of a tiger

whose black eyes stared out
from a tapestry of jungle vines,
emerald embroidered branches,

snakes like strings of topaz undulating
away as if lunging after the man
down the white florescent-lit hall.

I want to ask him now, as I sit on the couch,
rubbing my thumb over the needy brown upholstery,
watching lights go out

in the darkness I have inherited,
if there is something that made him need to cover

nakedness, like loneliness, in color.

At what point in his ten years alone
did he decide on that tattoo?
Was it in a moment like this

when night's charcoal shadow was closing,
like a hand, over the yellow light of lately lit apartment
  windows,
and the walls were going black,

in spite of the color, that he went
to have his body soldered by a solid reminder
that something could exist in absence?

That the unholiness of a body,
with its sting of solitude,
purple bruises, and blood-dark songs, could also be

the dark web of trees, a river, red flowers, green leaves spread
so wide they might shelter things, dew and pollen,
the rock-round backs of beetles, waking in the black to flap

their wings through heartless night, unafraid, so whenever he
  fell
back into himself, alone, in this room, he would land,
like that tiger, two paws dug into the solid earth, able

to look up through the lucid green embroidery
of the jungle's never-sleeping leaves, to find
even the inside of himself, still illuminated by stars.

Swan in the City

A gray one crosses my path. Flying
low through the smog of Los Angeles.
Of course, it might have been a goose,
or a lone mallard, lifting like a ship
into the clouds of the mid-city street lamps.
But I prefer to think it was a swan,
discolored with soot from our fair industrial city.
Past the reflective glass.
Past the coffee shops and face-down children
searching for quarters in the cracks of the sidewalk.
Quick over my car, ruffling the afternoon with her indefinite
feathers.
I like to think I conjured it
with all of my thoughts about swans.
A grey bird grieving for its natural habitat.
Swan with rain sliding down the doors of its eyes.
Swan with fish and feathers -
the intimate, North American size of its wings
and bright, black feet.
Like in Alaska, paring the sky open,
pushing the mist aside and sliding into the marshes.
My swan. Bringing me all
I have lost about mountains. All I have lost
from the bottle of wine. All
I have lost slinking through the city. Guilty
Virgin Mary. Mother may I? Amelia Earhart.
Its swollen bird breast navigating what I cannot
understand or see through. I am afraid of getting lost
without my GPS, my map, my cell-phone.
I am a dumb animal shot down

by beliefs. But the swan lifts her eight million
filaments of feather, her lost chicks, her dead brother,
the swamps of the north, the slick black mud of her birth,
the frozen tundra, out of whatever pool
she is swimming in this morning, and rises, rises,
rises into the skyline, past the buildings
that reflect her soaring. A quick slash of silhouette and shape
against the hardened glass.
A brief moment of motion and light.
Swan, without your flying through us
we would all fall out of the world.

Your Bear

My life was so lacking in bear.
–Hannah Gamble

When you were a child, it followed you;
though you didn't see it, you felt
it in every footprint. Rising
from your mother's shoes.
The neighbor's yard, so quiet
it must have had a bear in it.

Now you live in a city.
Cars move you
past the reflective windows.
In the blur you realize, you're missing
something. Suddenly you want
the big, un-embarrassed haunches
of a mammal with rough fur, lifting
its weight into the sunrise.

If you had your bear,
you could be honest again.
Admit you're tired of watching
the screen flash with code.
Figuring in taxes. Eating chicken
fully cooked.

When a bear looks at you, it sees
all the ways
your life is still lacking.
When you look at a bear, you see

branches full of birds.

Everything present tense again
and falling.

Come back it says.
The day is bright.
The forest is lonely.

It calls you, dangling
the dangerous pleasure
of bees.

Island

There is an island
where we are always locked out.

At quiet o'clock it reveals itself.
Island inside another island.

Waves tick by the hours,
changing the shape of a shore.

I have heard a caterpillar turn wet in her chrysalis
Kukui nut sweeten into ointment inside her shell.

Everything available and secret,
like in my grandmother's kitchen

before she died.

On the continent of discontent, I was always
dissolving into failures.

Wrapped in the geometry
of my misgivings.

In this silence the unfinished projects
evaporate. And I become

famous for my abalone colors.
An insect the sun wants to study.

When she was alive,
my grandmother could build

a house with her body.
Now the naked hour wraps me

in the pearl-rough music
of her sea.

The Pregnant Mare

has followed me into the Kukui nut grove.

The color of new continents, old island maps,
she is secretive as an acorn, mystery-heavy animal-hot.

In this continental drift I become an ear
pressed to a hush.

I worry she will smell
the danger in my hair, run away.

Instead, she comes closer,
nose pointed towards forest.

This moment is the color of silence.
Green swims through the trees.

Sunlight touches the husks
fallen on the floor.

I stand still as a grove. She
nudges her torso into my palm.

I remember my own mother.
The first separation. First communion.

Under the heat of the horse something moves.
Sunlit as an ocean. It widens before me.

A wordless body, touching
a wordless body.

Something from the invisible world
about to enter.

Our shared animal heart
beginning to grow.

Watching a YouTube Video of Elephants Mating

Everyone on safari went quiet.
Tourists stunned into stop motion.
A country away, I stopped the chaos
on my computer to watch them.

The male, with his enormous, two-tone member
entering the female. Slow. Careful,
like parking an impossibly expensive silver BMW
into a tight garage.

I'm lonely for that kind of knowledge.
Always trying to touch the flat
screen of this new century,
coming away with static.

I could be at a market, practicing Spanish,
while eating starfruit from the cart.
Instead, I hide from such pleasure.
Try to perfect my perfunctory parts.

But here it is now, on my phone.
That animal lust I've been trying to tame.
I could carry it in my pocket now,

as I buy more computer paper and glue.

I could look at it, in line, the tenderness
of the male elephant, using his trunk to stroke
the female while he mounts her
under the baobab tree.

Whatever kind of animal language we have forgotten,
the elephants keep reminding us.
No matter how estranged we feel, we carry

hurtling mines of the galaxy into the green

ecosystem of one another's bodies.
The enormous animal lust we follow.
The only reason we have
been able to survive.

Seeing the Howler Monkey Reach for Fruit I Am Reminded of the Time You Sent me a Naked Photo of Yourself from the Other Side of the World

Evening elongates its shadows pink
mangoes ache towards sweetness I wish
I were in ear-shot of myself

but I am elseward sniffing
The firmament sweats itself stupid
with desire.

In the summer your body looked
like this garden sugared with sweat
glistening in the shade of a book

Now the evening animals appear
familiar to me One lone howler hangs by his tail
from a tree Its torso a forest unfurling

he reaches for fruit
At this distance we are all silhouettes entering
the infinity of aloneness I remember

you once appeared under my skirt,
animaled across a bed with a head full of leaves
I responded naked as a solar system

showed you what I looked like
under my terror It was years ago
I'm still trying to live

honest with my instincts
When the mango dangles itself in front of me
I push my vandal fingers forward

Open-mouthed in moonlight
How can you blame me for wanting to pull
the entire jungle towards me?

The Simple Life

But it's not really. Out in this field, we watch
cows graze in the complicated grass.
Notice their ears, half-haloing their luminous eyes
as they look back at us. See what is growing in the pasture?
Lantana fall from the stem; blossoms undo
the careful geometry of their petals.
If you ate the wrong fruit now,
if you picked it up and rolled it in your mouth,
not knowing its poisons, you might collapse
into a million floating seeds of dandelion.
I've been watching the cows for hours
and I still can't tell you what weeds would stop
a heart or cure a fever.
But the cows know. From a thousand feet up,
we must look lazy, watching them chew
as the sun sets behind the pasture.
Simple people, doing nothing but giving
our attention to the glow
that leans into evening, part of some unspoken
knowledge that goes on and on and on.

The Art of Becoming a Sloth

"Tell them you have a new project. It will never be finished."
–Naomi Shihab Nye

First, slow yourself to the pace of a watercolor.
Move at the speed of a shadow stretching as you climb
over the heads of tourists, ribboning under the canopy.

Notice how the people move so quick below you.
Where is the fire?
What is the hurry is about?

Do not envy our ability to get so much done. Become
fully absorbed in the task of eating wet leaves.
Watching the sun heat a white mango.

When you sleep, do it very slowly,
counting snails as they slide
over the eyelids of your imagination.
They are in no hurry.
They have their homes on their backs.
Where would they go?

When it is quiet, listen
to the old music of wind through branches,
noting the landscape
as you take your slow body past the limits
of human comprehension.

You were born doing what it takes
Buddhists years to master,
giving your full attention to the moment
making your whole world one clarification
of flowers, sunlit beetles, the dazzle of green.

Even when the eagle attacks
or the jaguar opens its mouth to you,
these are forms of adoration.

You are necessary in the chain.
The hives of termites, that little movement
of ginger as it pushes through the soil, red
and spoiled with flavor.

When flies appear do not swat them away,

the more you let go of time,
the more time you have to watch
the claw-dangle of bats hanging upside down,
dreaming this world, sheltered as they are
by your watching. When you see the horsefly,
say thank you to the one who made them
shimmer like naked bracelets

balancing their bodies
on the momentary jewel case of leaves.

Love of Coconuts

When they ran out of saline solution,
nurses gave transfusions of coconut
water to soldiers in the Solomon Islands.
My friend told me this as she cut my hair. Told
me to use coconut oil instead of lotion,
coconut oil to pull impurities from my teeth.
Coconuts have the same pH balance as human blood.

So when I get to the shore of Oahu at five am,
the only woman walking through cold sand
without a surfboard and see the first
wild coconut of my adulthood, I think of her.

Imagine soldiers lying in cotton white beds
with coconuts infusing their blood,
the way pineapple infused the grape
in the pineapple wine I was drinking last night.
The way rain infuses the clouds overhead.
It's not yet sunrise, but already I see light
on the horizon, the bright passion-fruit yellow
of that star sliding its fingers out of night, infusing
my arm with flickers of what used to be real fire.

There is no such thing as independence.
No matter who you are, or where you come from,
nothing can live without being transformed,
translated, transfused by what lives near
the surface of the earth, making itself indispensable.

Even one morning on this shore
has translated me into ukulele music,
the smell of Frangipani ginger, Taro root.
Rain falls on the skin of the water.
This ocean came to us
from stardust and radiates still like the silver of a
sterling pendant my grandmother wore
before she died.

I hear laughter so old
it must be someone's grandmother,
somebody's starlight

sharing what she has been saving
from the time she burst open
and became an ocean, waiting to play
her silverfish--shark-whale-krill-sounding
guitar song just for me.

III

Solitary as a Swan

I couldn't tell if I was a bird
or half a silence.
The willow more like a lover than a tree,
it haunted the lake,
brushing her blue skin into ringlets.
I would paddle by watching
its spear-like leaves pet the water.
Marriage was like that,
I remembered. All the handsome men waiting
for war,
all the women letting them do small things for their backs.
I was a swan,
but I had been a woman. I had been a girl. I had been naked
as an egg, caressing
skin of wounded boys. In the garden, the sounds of clippers
clip herbs.
The lake quiet, like the inside of a trombone.
I would swim around the palace,
wary someone might recognize me.
But the servants were busy, going in or coming out,
a horse looked bored,
and I would turn away. Shadows disorganizing the water,
scattering owls over the edge of reflections.
All of those skulls
and tufts fur from foraged mice,
the little bones, delicate as the China forks we used
to clean our teeth.
I didn't know how happy I was
to be a swan, living
in the pure hush
of my own mirrors.
The deranged heads of flowers bowing to me.
Nature always knows
who we are.

Gametes. Godheads.
Moments melting from our singular brightness back
into the jade
unknown.

When We Named It

The hunter moon hung

its horn from a cloud.

Moss glowed on rock.

Men rose

from the rivers. Green.

On the banks of the Seine, the stag muddied its antlers.

We drank beside it. Ripple-shine, star-gardens,

our hands knifing

stone into fish, fins, faces.

Now we stand

under the old statues, asking

where have they lead us?

The people we once were,

carving up the earth into houses and towers,

cities and catacombs?

All the changes we have worshiped.

All the gods we animals have made.

Unfinished Love Poem with Crows

You confessed wanting
to fly into me,
the way a shaman flies into things.
Black wing of the heart.
Old feathers of a crow.

It is summer and we are driving
toward Santa Cruz.
Rain pulls moss from the branches
of oak trees,
their trunks dark as the shadows hidden
under a woman's dress.

Pull over to the side of the road and hold me.
I want to believe you,
that the darkness closed away
in the spot
between your eyelids and your eyes,
is a crow.

Pull me towards you
like a bird lifting its weight
into the branches of a tree,
figure breaking the empty air.
Black stitches on a quilt holding earth
firmly against the sky.

Advice from a Bird

Listen, one day the river will become ugly.
The fish will lose their purse full of comets.
The deer slice open
their beautiful, rounded tongues.
Your mate will go out to fish
and never return.

There will be arguments swimming in your mouth,
always. Women walking by themselves
at night trying not to swallow the moon.
Listen. You must do what you must.
Eat where the food grows.
Drink when it rains.

There are forests humming
on the other side of fear,
poisoned mushrooms in the meadows of love.
If a hunter comes, pretend to be ugly.
If a photographer wants to take your picture, smile
and pretend to be daylight.

Land on the leaves.
Land on the stamen of little yellow flowers.

Do not break your wings
when you come in for a landing.
The mouth is beautiful
only so many hours of the day.

Keep it closed and look up.

Get ready to repeat your tragedy
into the ears of the stars.

Vermin

I never told anyone about the affair.

That night, after it was over,
after the thing had ended and he had gone back
to his girlfriend,

I came home and found a note from my landlord.
Got your message about the rat, it said,
slipped some poison under the house.

I threw the note away,
thought any death was cruel,
then went to bed early

to dream about a man sleeping
next to a woman
who wasn't me.

When I woke it was to the sound
of the rat clawing
under the floorboards.

He must have been hungry.
Eating dirt from the bottom of the house.
Chewing up wood. A small thing with claws

like human hands, wanting to hold anything
it could find to fill a belly.
I knew he was eating what would kill him.

Later, when I got up again before dawn,
it was his dying I heard. His stifled voice coming
through the slats of the vent.

His rat heart going black as a boot heel.
The heat of his body stinking
through my floor boards,

like the smell of sweat left over in a bed.
I listened carefully. This cry in the suburbs.
How I woke to hear the rat consuming its own death,

how I learned anything can get so hungry
it will gnaw, even at the darkest parts
of someone else's house.

The Body Blisters

Breaks into heat rash. Sweat.

I cannot escape my incarcerated animal.

My skin swelters rough. Prickles under ivory dresses.

I become shear

as an egg. Shocked into the sharp buzzing

of afternoon. Fur-less, I am bruised

by each fall. Stung by the hive of afternoons

in the open. My lungs alive

with running. I have no hooves

against this mountain's raw thistle.

Instead, rapture.

I hold my head inside the green thrills.

Still.

I follow. Still, I tell it. I'm not ready

for the tooth and fire ants and boiling lakes.

I become human with this first music.

I become human

from my discomfort with this world.

Leather

I like driving too fast on the freeway
to get here where liquor is cheap

and ready to sting me awake.
Bad decision broken down by margarita mix
and lapped down with salt.

Forget the flowers.
Give me an excuse to sit
at a barstool with strangers
pecking at their phones. The waitress brings them
tequila and Coke.

I want things manmade.
The leather-stripped cow and tooled into a high heel the color
  of sex.
More animal than even animal.

I watch the men pull
nameless fish out of the ocean,
their silver bodies flapping in the sand.

Glad I'm not the pelicans
on the horizon hysterically caught
up in a line not meant for them.

Later I'll meditate. Consider the biodiversity of this
butterfly sanctuary. Apologize to mother
Earth; re-plant some flowers in her rainforest.

But today, give me another Chiliguaro.
Split the lip of the pineapple. Queen bitch
of this jungle. My wallet made of dumb cow.

I'm sick of trying
not to be a predator.
Trying not to smile as I kill
the spider
who has crawled into my hand.

Murder Swan

(Halszkaraptor Escuilliei)

In the beginning, I walked on clawed feet, carving
fish from a stream. Hissed

a black song. Now the world is more civilized. We carve

minarets. Sphinx the body of a predator out of sand to protect
us from storm.

Every day, evolution tries to bargain with me. Be more
beautiful.
Soft as a teapot. A cloud.

But nature cannot take back what it has already given.

I break my kill across the canvas.

Swallow small fish
and frogs from the marshes.

No matter how beautiful we become,
we have all broken something
to get here.

Left claws cracked in our wake.
Fed our bodies
on the salt death of crabs.

IV

Eclipse

The Swan points north,
stars drink
in the mouth of the Little Bear

no matter how old we get
night takes us back
to our place
in a constellation
of seeds

glommed around the root
growling ourselves open.
Night cat. Cricket.

The nocturnes
of moths
alighting on unlit lamp posts.

When the eclipse occurs
I remember
the privacy of the first horses

how they fed
on night flowers.

Before the stars
came out to howl
like wolves
and God appeared
to turn on

            the searchlight
of the moon.

Questions for a Search Engine

If only you could sing me a star song
like the bards used to do.

Layers of history sediment over. Languages lose themselves.
Under the man-made lake something lurks.

If only you could predict the past
like a soothsayer. Break open like oracle bones.

On this side of the tea leaves, the flowers
keep falling. Tell me what animal

my grandmother has become
now she blossoms celestial side.

I dream forests walking towards us.
What do these images signify?

Tell me why the cavemen printed
their hands on walls. What were they trying to say?

Tell me how this star-song ends. Tell me
what was written on the back of their eyes?

At the Alaskan Native Heritage Center

For your safety, we ask you not try to understand
the history of our death.
Watch instead the kayak resurrect itself
from the stump of the tree and become the totem of self,
the bones of the grey whale reassemble themselves
against the silt of Lake Tiulana.
Meet and greet with the thousand naked shells
crushed into the mouth of a gull.
Tours start at the tip of the walrus' tusk
and follow round the curve of the wind.
We invite you to meet the baleen
where it becomes the size of a small sunset
inside the planet of the mammal's flesh.
Come see the scheduled rise
and fall of a culture.
The eleven O'clock history of bones, beached on a blue shore.
Here the salmon start their native dance.
They swish into the streams, then exit.
Their glasses hang loose from their grey scales
as they nod approval to every rock
painted under water.
When the bear emerges, they are cool
as New Yorkers, stepping onto an old bus.
What do they care about death, here
where everything moves
from one daylight to another?
And when you arrive at the last drop of sun,
you too will cherish it, like a krill cherishes
the grapefruit sized opening in the mouth of a beluga.

When you leave this place, nothing will change.
Except the shadows will turn back to eagles in the water,
and the raven will again give birth and swallow the sun.

Surrendering to Alaska

Up here, hunger forms
a higher order.

Blizzards cover bone.
Tectonic plates
grow glaciers and crack.

We shift. We surrender.
We harden
into our stories.

In this new hush, I ask the world
what it thinks of us.

Fir needles fall.
A grizzly catches its salmon.
The sky rotates its answer.

Before we can become entirely spirit,
we must become entirely wilderness.

Let death come.
Let snow fall.
Let silence hold us

in its thin shell
fragile and perfect as an egg.

Blue Fish in February

Our birthdays collide, two fish swimming
in opposite directions.

The constellation of Pisces slinks through
the southern hemisphere.

Your figure rotates behind a curtain.
Moth trapped against screen door of reminiscence.

I walk the fields. When I cannot sleep,
stars slip
in and out of consciousness.

This morning I wrote they are fish
disappearing into a season that hazed endless.
Tonight, they return.

If you were here,
I would tattoo my hand
over the blue whale under your shirt.

Once the moon shimmered into white rabbit.
The clothing of Yeats woven
from dreams.

I see it as something different now.
Stars, like the scale of koi
slide apart into separate hemispheres.

The hills tiger blue

into distance.
This blistered shadow all I have left.

Memory of a tattoo sinking
one year deeper
into the shadow of your chest.

Life Cycle of the Salmon

When we were fish,
the men put their hands
into our clear glass house,

their spears into our pink,
blood-splattered sides.

We didn't mind.
Our bodies were inconsequential.

Clothes of scales. Moments of craving
for the river.

If one of us died, we leapt
into the body of a stag

and rode the next rain
back down.

But last night the wind rocked
our house. We could not sleep.

Death washed onto the shore,
rotting ship of bones interlocked with twine.

Someone's laughter dragged away
by the movement of a net.

Now I wake and find my stories
broken outside of the body.

Overhead the swans riot,
windows open with their black feet.

When I wake you are still
dreaming next to me.

Animal separated by skin.
Reconnected with language.

When I wake, God comes as a glimpse of bear,
each bird in its mouth, a house

torn apart by the blue teeth
of the sky.

My New God Plays the Ukulele

Knows how to mend
the strings.
Is stuck on this island with me,
gets hungry at regular intervals.
Does not check their clock.

My new God is deaf to praise. Lives
in a world of silent sinners.
Loves the Brazilian Cardinal. Lusts
after the color green.

My new God worships honeybees. Keeps
track of their numbers.
Is replanting milk thistle and clover.
Is protecting scorpions and snakes.
Whistles silence like a seahawk
waiting overhead in the trees.

My new God wastes mangoes. Wastes
hours they invented sleeping
in hammocks
with a cat curled in their lap.
Lets so many things rot and die
and come back as sapling
or dream.

My new God likes
to swim in the river. Race
the boats like a doll's porpoise. Appears
to us in the body of a stranded whale.
Wears the fins of a shark.
Cuts you like coral.

My new God fattens
our hands with honeyberry.
Plumps up the skin with bee-sting.
Talks to us in blister.
Is trying to get our attention.

My new God breaks
the tree with lighting, the sidewalk
with seedling,
heals the sunburn
and every scar.

Calls to us in the lonely voice
of a grey-eyed loon.
My new God is everywhere.
Reflects itself in the shimmer of pond water,
enters the body
through a wound.

Soursop

> *"I've heard space changes you. I want to see how it will change me."*
> *–Jeff Bezos on using his wealth to build rockets.*

I understand, El Jefe,
why you must build your rockets
to nowhere. For the hungry
we have with us always, but you
are temporary. Small as a fever.
How can you resist the temptation
to see a moment of largess spinning,
pear-tilted. Alive. I too have spent
too much on myself. Shopping
at the local stand, buying
exotic fruit, I saw a woman
who looked like me reaching
for a white mango.
Across her arm a black rose tattoo blossomed,
and that changed me in ways I can't describe.
I let my old life die, and still
I go on living.
Starting over, like a flower stolen
from a flower shop
that survives on a counter. And I can
tell you, all moments are the same
moment. The moment
we become conscious
of what we are holding.
Here is the inside of a green soursop.
Here is the face of the entire universe

falling open in my hand.
What will you do next, Jeff,
now that you've seen it?
The green world spinning, without you.
What do any of us tiny deities do
when we're no longer afraid to die?

V

Catacombs

This is how we remember
what we love.

Build a city
over it.

Rearrange skulls
into fountains,

bones
into tourist attractions.

We see ourselves ushered
into the underworld.

Ask something to hold
still.

But even the statues remind us

the moon
has lost her antlers,

what started the world
will end it again.

And what loves us, will love us so hard
it will bury

its bright
in our bones.

A Walk through the Parking Lot at Midnight

The worm goes its whole life
without owning a face.

One angular stream of light,
it eats through darkness alone.

Tonight cities sleep underground
waiting to be rediscovered.

Atoms lie pressed
by the weight of cars.

I walk through the parking lot, moving
from one sky to another.

I wanted to live forever, but
metal rusts, plastic melts thin.

Each atom swirls through the space of my body
like a salmon swimming through Alaska.

Carbon atoms bumping into each other in a stream.

This night is a picture of the brain.
Neurons fire through the darkness like meteors.

I walk from one night to another.
Moon of the skull orbiting the earth,

and inside my body, the bones shimmering in the darkness
like stars.

Let

Let the stars fall.
Let the newspapers loosen their ink.
Let money turn itself backward into the branches of trees.

Let the deer walk the streets unharmed. And the arrows fall
from stars.
Let morning glories reclaim each tenement,
vines soothe the city back to sleep.

Let the bus break down in clover.
Let the robots rest on the road.

Let the last pumpkin rot forward 'til it opens
into tiny umbrellas, ribbed with translucent spores.

Our old world was written in the stars.
Our new will appear through fungi, turning
the dead to food.

In this steel hearted century,
in this wishbone-broken city,
throw everything you have towards the ground.

Let dirt and darkness translate
our past into new seeds.

How Animals Write Poetry

Smell how I carve
my scent into the forest,

make the birds hear
my claws, clattering,

over the frost-
white page of morning.

In winter I suffer.
In spring I mother

a new replica of my fur,
edit the ticks out of their hinds.

Artist or animal,
it's all the same text.

Creatures, we write
our history fast, then forget,

leaving replicas
of our skeletons

as we disappear
into snow.

Don't Write

"If trees could speak, they wouldn't."
–Dorianne Laux

Solitude enters the city like a sunken sun.
Sadness of doves silvering the fences.

The day closes its mouth, looks into a lake.
Shadows have come all this way to curl onto your chest.

You want to capture something.
Say it back to whatever is breathing this night air.

But the mouth of the universe will not be filled
by your tiny lexicon.

Something happens in the star gardens above us.
Donate your tongue to its unfolding. Become

the flight in the solitude of doves.
The green in the silence of trees.

Ursa Major

During summer I am full
of expectations.

I eat through the woods
so I can sleep into my death undisturbed.

Time is a river.

Whatever I have in my mouth used to be alive,
and I killed it with my teeth.

A man walks into the room. I rub
my scent on his neck.

In my den I lie
like one weighted with honey.

A group of bears is a sleuth,
from the Latin *to move slow.*

If I live starrily as a bear,
I can feel a constellation forming.

Ursa Major, following the Northern Cross,
the neck of a swan stretches towards infinity.

Here I am, on a map of the sky.
Lifting my nose towards the sugar of Polaris.

Wood smoke lifts from the fires, offering
its blown-open translucence of seeds.

Ode to the (Current) North Star

All night
the North Star governs our lives.
A cosmic lighthouse, guiding
sailors and the astronauts. Making poets
look up, quiet.
But in 13,000 years
the Earth will tilt, and we'll all turn
to birds again.
Polaris will be overthrown by new hungers.
By then we'll have been recycled
into oceans and water bottles.
New generations drinking our old tears.
It feels small and quotidian
to be alive. The way the stars align
every night making something
as ordinary as a belt for Orion,
or a dipper anyone can drink from.
A big bear and a little one
pointing their noses
in the direction of the night's cold
pollen. As if the sun is just one stain
of honeycomb,
ministering us around and around,
little lost cygnets
following the tail end
of a constellation
as we circle towards
something.
But who can say what

we follow, looking up
into that featherless sky.

Acknowledgements

"Why Do We Pretend God Isn't an Animal?" was originally published by *New York Quarterly*, in their anthology, *Without a Doubt.*

"Spring Delayed," and "The Pregnant Mare" were originally published in *Pawling Living.*

"Dear Iceberg" was originally published in *Quill and Pen.*

"Bear Poem" was originally published in *River Heron Review.*

"How to Identify the Body of God" was originally published in *Wild Roof Journal.*

"Unfinished Love Poem with Crows" was originally published in *Melusine.*

"Vermin" was originally published in *Poet Lore.*

"Tattoos on Young Women in Spring" was originally published in *Rattle.*

"Murder Swan" was originally published in *The Fourth River: Salvage* Edition.

"Advice from a Bird" was originally published in *Whale Road Review.*

"Love of Coconuts" was originally published in *Pine Row.*

"Blue Fish in February" was originally published in *Pirene's Fountain.*

"The Jungle Tattoo" was originally published in *BloodLotus Poetry Journal*.

"How to Deal with Mortality" was originally published in *Peacock Journal*.

"Swan in the City" was originally published in *The Chiron Review*.

"Ursa Major" was originally published in *Snapdragon*

"A Walk through the Parking Lot at Midnight" was originally published in *The Cincinnati Review* and was winner of the Robert and Adele Schiff Poetry Award.

"The Pregnant Mare" and "Spring Delayed" appeared in *Pawling Living*.

The following poems were awarded the Pangea Prize as a collection. "Territorial Boundaries," "Eclipse" (originally titled "The Basket of the Sky Gluts Itself on Stars"), "When we First Named It" (originally titled "When the Moon Had Antlers"), "Catacombs," "Question for a Search Engine," "Don't Write," "Ode to the Current North Star."

*   *   *   *   *

I owe huge thanks to so many people, places, poems, poets and books on how to write poetry.

I want to express deep gratitude to some of my teachers – Kim Addonizio, Brendan Constantine, Jack Grapes, Sally Ashton and others who have taught me how to write and craft poetry.

Endless thanks to those who have helped me edit these poems, especially Kelly Grace Thomas whose friendship and moral as well as artistic support has buoyed me during so many storms. To Kelly Cressio-Moeller and David Perez who used to trade poems and feedback with me over coffee in San Jose during my formative years – you helped form me.

Much appreciation to those who gave me feedback on the manuscript – Diane Lockward, Kim Malinowski, Sherre Vernon, Kika Dorsey and Alicia Elkort – all writers I treasure and admire.

Infinite gratitude to Hank Hudepohl and Pine Row Press for choosing to publish this collection.

My thanks and deepest love to Allen Rubinstein who agreed to move to Costa Rica with me, who proof-read many versions of this book, and who has given me the kind of love all of us need to thrive.

Also, much love to my long-time friend Melsa, who encouraged my early writing during the years when I first started this project.

Finally, to all the members, past and future, of The Poetry Salon. The community we are building together is the reason I do this work. It is also my deepest reward.

Notes

"Dear Iceberg" is modeled after the poem "Notes on a Nonexistent Expedition to the Himalayas" by Wislawa Szymborska.

"At the Alaskan Native Heritage Center" was composed using imagery from the museum as well as words and phrases from the brochure distributed at the time.

“Why do we pretend god isn’t an animal/ a beetle, antlered for the hoisting of stars” comes from Brendan Constantine’s poem, “Litany.”

“This world keeps remaking itself – without me” comes from a poem by Kelly Grace Thomas called “Without Me or Infertility" that was sent to the author of this book privately, and has not yet appeared in print.

“My life was so lacking in bear” comes from Hannah Gamble’s poem “Growing a Bear.”

“The Art of Becoming a Sloth” takes its title from Naomi Shihab Nye’s poem “The Art of Disappearing.”

The accompanying quote also comes from the same poem. "Love of Coconuts" was inspired by something the poet, Julie Van Brasch told me while cutting my hair.

“When we Named it” and “Catacombs” were inspired by research into the origins of the city of Paris. Originally the city was inhabited by the British Celtic tribe of the Parisi who lived along the Seine. Over centuries, the region became more urbanized and eventually overcrowded with the bones of the dead who were buried there. The city built the catacombs, which are a major tourist attraction today.

“Murder Swan” is inspired by an ancient fossil found in Mongolia that suggests there was once a dinosaur shaped like a swan. Ed Yong, of The Atlantic gave this prehistoric creature the name “murder swan.”

“Eclipse” makes reference to a Swan pointing north. That refers to the constellation of The Swan. Within that constellation is the smaller constellation of the Northern Cross. The tail of the swan is marked by the star Daneb.

“Live Cycle of the Salmon” and the other poems that reference Alaska were inspired by my honeymoon at Anchorage and Resurrection Bay, during which I read Margaret Craven’s book, *I Heard the Owl Call My Name*. The book references the Kwakiutle people and their beliefs about the Salmon as a symbol of both life-giving abundance and the cyclical nature of death and rebirth.

“Soursop” refers to a type of fruit that grows in the tropics. The quote comes from Jeff Bezos, founder of Amazon, who used some of his vast fortune to build a private rocket ship to take him and other wealthy patrons into space. The poem also calls Jeff, “El Jefe” which is the Spanish language colloquialism for “boss.”

“Let” was inspired loosely on Linda Gregg’s poem, “Let Birds.”

“If trees could speak, they wouldn’t” comes from Dorianne Laux’s poem “The Life of Trees.”

Ursa Major is a constellation that translates into English as Great She-Bear. Within this constellation is The Big Dipper. The Big Dipper opens to Polaris, the current North Star, which is also part of the constellation of Ursa Minor, the Little Bear.

“Ode to the Current North Star" is inspired by learning that the North Star Polaris will someday not be the North Star. Scientists believe that as the Earth rotates, Daneb will take its place as the new North Star. Daneb marks the tail end of the constellation called The Swan.

About the Poet

TRESHA FAYE HAEFNER is an award-winning author, creativity coach and speaker. One of the few people to hold a master's degree in humanistic psychology, with a specialization in creativity studies, Tresha uses research-based methods to help others develop their most authentic creative abilities, both for the sake of artistic expression and personal well-being. She often tells her classes that she began writing only so she could have the credentials to teach workshops to other innovative writers and poets.

Tresha has been an active member and teacher at California Poets in the Schools, helped to curate the CPITS *Anthology of Lesson Plans, Poetry Crossing*, and has been a grant recipient through the Los Angeles Department of Cultural Affairs Artist-In-Residence program.

Tresha has studied with innovative poets such as Kim Addonizio, Sally Ashton, Ellen Bass, Gabrielle Calvacoressi, Brendan Constantine, Matthew Dickman, Jack Grapes, Suzanne Lummis, Eloise Klein Healy, Naomi Shihab-Nye, and founder of the Poetry Depths Mystery School, Kim Rosen. Her own work has been published in several journals, including *BloodLotus, The Cincinnati Review Fourth River, Hunger Mountain, Pirene's Fountain, Poet Lore, Prairie Schooner,* and *Rattle*. She is the recipient of the 2011 Robert and Adele Schiff Poetry Prize, the 2011 Alien Sloth Sex Award, a 2015 and 2020 Pushcart nomination, and a 2019 Best of the Net nomination. She's the author of two chapbooks, *Tattoos on Young Women in Spring* (Poetry Salon Press) and *Take This Longing* (Finishing Line Press).

After living in Costa Rica for three years, she now lives in North Carolina with her husband, Allen Rubinstein, who writes about film and history for *Cinema of the 70s Magazine*.

Advance Praise for *When the Moon Had Antlers*

Tresha Faye Haefner's new collection of poems, *When the Moon Had Antlers,* made me pause with breathlessness wanting to underline each stunning line. From a boy who wanted to reach out and touch an iceberg to blackbirds falling from an Arkansas sky, these engaging poems surprise and glimmer with energy and thoughtfulness—*a crab hides in the arrogance of shade*, a shore that *translated me into/ukulele music and the smell of frangipani ginger, the Taro root.* Throughout the collection, Haefer unites us with the environment and with something larger: *My new god worships honeybees…Reflects itself in the shimmer of pond water,/Enters the body/through a wound.* These are poems we need and need to listen to, where ecopoetics, melancholy, and spirituality hold hands and connect us to a world where there are *people who will hug us/then melt back into the night. When the Moon Had Antlers* is poetry that helps us *feel* again and understand how *we pocket our sadness*. Let these beautiful poems help us *connect/our bodies back to the stars;* let these poems help us *remember/what we love.*

–Kelli Russell Agodon, *Dialogues with Rising Tides* (Copper Canyon Press)

*   *   *   *   *

I really am quite blown away by Tresha Haefner's new collection *When The Moon Had Antlers*, not only by her brave bolts of imagination and the forceful contretemps of her unexpected insights that range from personal confessional to environmental visionary. For certainly this poet interprets the world with sensitivity, joy, and a devoted flair for invention. But please note, as well, the master craft hands at work here. These taut, image-rich lines are lean and muscular in syntax while lush in language and a poet's spirit faithfully surrendered to and embraced by the thriving cosmic, green, and animal landscapes around her. Because: "Anything to end this aloneness, / anything to connect / our bodies back to the stars."

–Michelle Bitting (*Nightmares & Miracles*, a *Kirkus Reviews* 2022 Best of Indie)

*   *   *   *   *

In many ways, *When the Moon Had Antlers* feels like a recentering of civilization, a disruption of progress in order to remember what makes it all worth it. Both lyrical and deeply rooted, this collection of work makes the reader step outside, away from the loud of cities into the crisp and contemplative quiet of the wilderness and all it offers. Here, nature manifests in its many forms - a tattoo on the body, a reigniting of the lust within, a scratching at the floorboards, hope. Here, nature invades the every day as question and answer - it is what makes us human, and it is what makes us long for ourselves. A journey at times beautiful, others visceral and violent, this debut collection is a must read from a poet who has much to offer the world, especially in the age of technology.

–Deshawn McKinney, author of *father forgive me* (Black Sunflowers Poetry Press)

For those who named the stars
and for those who still plant the seeds

www.ingramcontent.com/pod-product-compliance
Lightning Source LLC
LaVergne TN
LVHW010627100826
845148LV00014B/3148